MARS

by Emma Bassier

Cody Koala
An Imprint of Pop!
popbooksonline.com

abdobooks.com

Published by Pop!, a division of ABDO, PO Box 398166, Minneapolis, Minnesota 55439. Copyright © 2021 by POP, LLC. International copyrights reserved in all countries. No part of this book may be reproduced in any form without written permission from the publisher. Pop!™ is a trademark and logo of POP, LLC.

Printed in the United States of America, North Mankato, Minnesota.

102020
012021

THIS BOOK CONTAINS RECYCLED MATERIALS

Cover Photos: NASA, Mars; iStockphoto, background
Interior Photos: NASA, 1 (Mars), 5 (top), 5 (bottom left), 9, 16–17, 19 (top), 19 (bottom left), 19 (bottom right), 20; iStockphoto, 1 (background), 5 (bottom right), 6; NASA/JPL-Caltech/University of Arizona/Science Source, 10; Shutterstock Images, 13, 14 (Mars), 14 (Sun)

Editor: Alyssa Krekelberg
Series Designer: Colleen McLaren

Library of Congress Control Number: 2020940276
Publisher's Cataloging-in-Publication Data
Names: Bassier, Emma, author.
Title: Mars / by Emma Bassier
Description: Minneapolis, Minnesota : POP!, 2021 | Series: Planets | Includes online resources and index
Identifiers: ISBN 9781532169090 (lib. bdg.) | ISBN 9781532169458 (ebook)
Subjects: LCSH: Mars (Planet)--Juvenile literature. | Planets--Juvenile literature. | Solar system--Juvenile literature. | Milky Way--Juvenile literature. | Space--Juvenile literature.
Classification: DDC 523.43--dc23

Hello! My name is

Cody Koala

Pop open this book and you'll find QR codes like this one, loaded with information, so you can learn even more!

Scan this code* and others like it while you read, or visit the website below to make this book pop.

popbooksonline.com/mars

*Scanning QR codes requires a web-enabled smart device with a QR code reader app and a camera.

Table of Contents

Chapter 1
Next to Earth 4

Chapter 2
The Red Planet 8

Chapter 3
Long Seasons 12

Chapter 4
Exploring Mars 18

Making Connections 22
Glossary 23
Index 24
Online Resources 24

Chapter 1

Next to Earth

Mars is the fourth planet from the Sun. It is small and red. Mars is approximately half the size of Earth.

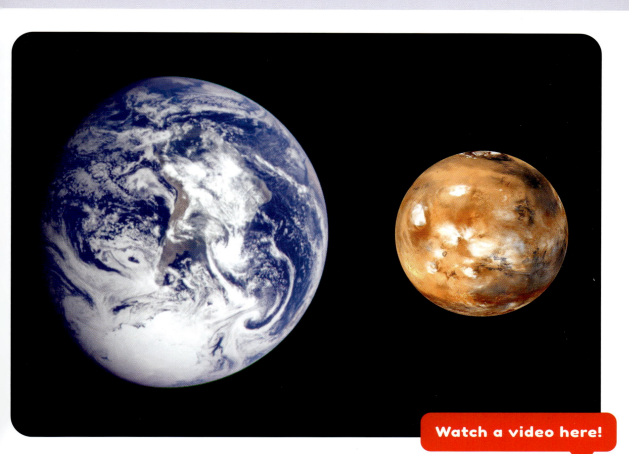

Watch a video here!

Mars is one of eight planets in the **solar system**. The Sun is at the center of the solar system. All the planets **orbit** it.

Mars travels in an egg-shaped path around the Sun.

Chapter 2

The Red Planet

Mars is a rocky planet. Its surface is dusty. Its red color comes from **iron** in the soil. The surface has peaks, **craters**, and canyons.

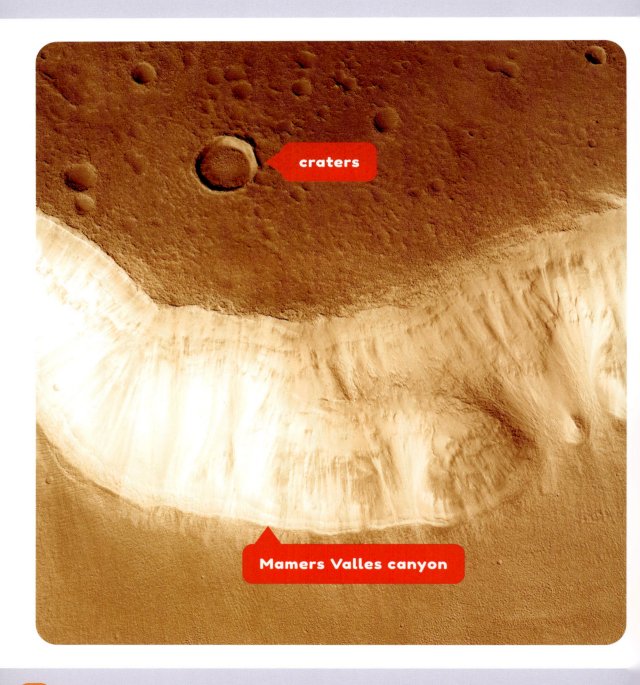

Mars has seasons and weather. But Mars does not have air that people can breathe. And its **atmosphere** is too thin to trap much heat from the Sun. So temperatures change quickly there.

> Temperatures on Mars can be as cold as –225 degrees Fahrenheit (–107°C).

Chapter 3

Long Seasons

One lap around the Sun is the length of one year. It takes Mars 687 Earth days to **orbit** the Sun.

Mars

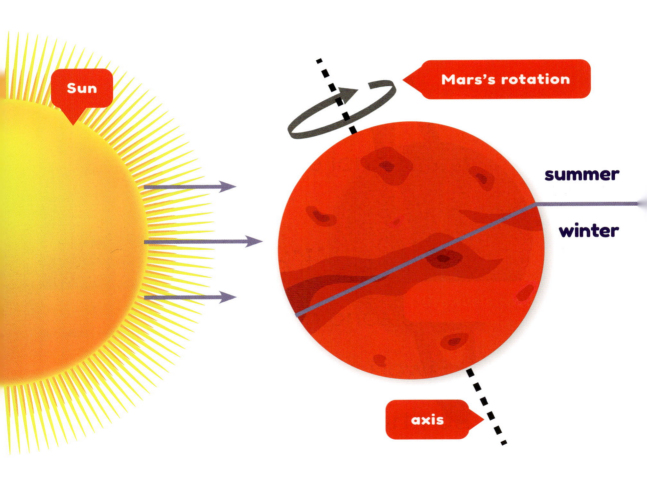

Mars spins on its **axis**. One spin is the length of one day. A day on Mars lasts 24.6 hours. This is similar to the length of a day on Earth.

Mars's axis is slightly tilted. The tilt causes seasons. Warmer seasons happen on parts of Mars that tilt

In winter, Mars has frost.

toward the Sun. Colder seasons happen on parts of Mars that tilt away.

Chapter 4

Exploring Mars

Scientists have explored Mars. It is the only planet they have sent rovers to. Rovers are robots that move across the ground.

Complete an activity here!

Rovers have taken pictures and collected rocks. These things help scientists learn more about Mars. They show that Mars once had water on its surface.

Scientists think that long ago, basic life could have lived on Mars.

Making Connections

Text-to-Self

Scientists study rocks on Mars to learn about the planet's history. What is your favorite thing to learn about? How do you learn about it?

Text-to-Text

Have you read other books about planets? How are those planets similar to or different from Mars?

Text-to-World

Mars is very dusty and dry. Can you think of some places on Earth that are like this?

Glossary

atmosphere – the layers of gases that surround a planet.

axis – an imaginary line that runs through the middle of a planet, from top to bottom.

crater – a deep hole in the ground.

iron – a type of metal that rusts in moist air.

orbit – to follow a rounded path around another object.

solar system – a collection of planets and other space material orbiting a star.

Index

atmosphere, 11

axis, 14, 15–16

iron, 8

rovers, 18, 21

seasons, 11, 16–17

solar system, 7

Sun, 4, 7, 11, 12, 14, 17

weather, 11

Online Resources

popbooksonline.com

Thanks for reading this Cody Koala book!

Scan this code* and others like it in this book, or visit the website below to make this book pop!

popbooksonline.com/mars

*Scanning QR codes requires a web-enabled smart device with a QR code reader app and a camera.